BEST OF MARCH MADNESS

MARCH MADNESS MEN'S SUPERSTARS

BY LUKE HANLON

abdobooks.com

Published by Abdo Publishing, a division of ABDO, PO Box 398166, Minneapolis, Minnesota 55439.

Printed in the United States of America, North Mankato, Minnesota.
102025
012026

Cover Photos: Sporting News Archive/Getty Images, Chuck Burton/AP Images, Sporting News Archive/Getty Images
Interior Photos: Bettmann/Getty Images, 4–5, 24; Rich Clarkson/NCAA Photos/Getty Images, 7, 8, 10, 14, 17, 19, 44; Bill Streator/AP Images, 12–13; Manny Millan/Sports Illustrated/Getty Images, 20–21; Andy Hayt/Sports Illustrated/Getty Images, 23; Charles Arbogast/AP Images, 26; John Biever/Sports Illustrated/Getty Images, 28–29; Craig Jones/Getty Images Sport/Getty Images, 30; Elsa/Getty Images Sport/Getty Images, 33; Chuck Burton/AP Images, 35; Chris Trotman/Getty Images Sport/Getty Images, 36–37; Bill Shettle/Cal Sport Media/AP Images, 39; Chris Steppig/NCAA Photos/Getty Images, 40; Jamie Sabau/NCAA Photos/Getty Images, 42; Streeter Lecka/Getty Images Sport/Getty Images, 45

Editor: Dalton Rains
Series Designer: Ebonee Estrella

Library of Congress Control Number: 2025939873

Publisher's Cataloging-in-Publication Data

Names: Hanlon, Luke, author.
Title: March Madness men's superstars / by Luke Hanlon
Description: Minneapolis, Minnesota: Abdo Publishing, 2026 | Series: Best of March Madness | Includes online resources and index.
Identifiers: ISBN 9781098298180 (lib. bdg.) | ISBN 9798384931980 (ebook)
Subjects: LCSH: Basketball--Juvenile literature. | College sports--Juvenile literature. | Basketball--Tournaments--United States--Juvenile literature. | College sports--United States--History--Juvenile literature. | NCAA Basketball Tournament--Juvenile literature. | March Madness (National Collegiate Athletic Association)--Juvenile literature.
Classification: DDC 796.32363--dc23

TABLE OF CONTENTS

CHAPTER ONE

BIRD VS. MAGIC

Earvin "Magic" Johnson received a pass behind the half-court line. The 6-foot, 8-inch Michigan State point guard immediately sensed an opportunity. Johnson heaved a long pass toward the basket for an alley-oop. Not so fast. Larry Bird had read the play perfectly. The Indiana State forward leaped into the air and stole the pass. Just before he fell out of bounds, Bird dished the ball to a teammate to keep the play alive.

The crowd buzzed. More than 15,000 fans were in Salt Lake City, Utah, for the championship game of the 1979 National Collegiate Athletic Association (NCAA) men's basketball tournament. Fans had been hoping to see Johnson and Bird face off all year. The charismatic Johnson, a sophomore, played with energy and flair. Meanwhile, the more-serious Bird had all but carried Indiana State to the title game.

Indiana State's Larry Bird, *left*, averaged 27.2 points and 5.2 assists per game in the 1979 NCAA Tournament.

The senior had earned a Naismith Trophy as national player of the year.

MAGIC MAN

Johnson grew up in Lansing, Michigan. As a kid, he took a basketball everywhere he went. Constant practice helped him become a star at Everett High School. Awed by the 15-year-old's skill, a local sports reporter described Johnson as "magic." The nickname stuck.

Johnson had the body of a power forward. But he also could dribble and pass like a point guard. So he ran Everett's offense. Nobody knew how to stop him. As a senior in 1977, Johnson led his team to a state championship. Then he headed to nearby East Lansing, Michigan, for college.

When Johnson arrived at Michigan State, the Spartans' last trip to the NCAA Tournament had been 19 seasons earlier. Things quickly turned around. As a freshman in 1977–78, Johnson led the country in assists while lifting the Spartans to the Elite Eight. He increased his assist numbers as a sophomore. Then he went on a tear in the 1979 NCAA Tournament. In each of Michigan State's first four games, Johnson recorded at least 13 points and 10 assists.

In the Final Four, the Spartans faced Pennsylvania. Johnson dominated, missing only one of his 10 attempts

Earvin "Magic" Johnson (33) averaged 11.3 assists per game in Michigan State's first four 1979 NCAA Tournament games.

from the field. He finished the game with 29 points, 10 rebounds, and 10 assists. The triple-double lifted the Spartans to a 101–67 win and their first appearance in the national championship game.

LARRY LEGEND

Bird was born and raised in French Lick, Indiana. It was a small town with a population of barely more than 2,000 people. High school basketball served as French Lick's main form of entertainment. Massive crowds came to watch Bird play at Springs Valley High School. Locals even offered to drive his parents to his games, since his parents couldn't afford a car of their own.

Bird made 16 of his 19 field goal attempts in the 1979 NCAA semifinals.

About 4,000 people showed up to watch Bird play his final home game at Springs Valley. He then headed to the powerhouse team at Indiana to play college basketball. However, after less than a month on campus, he left the school. Bird ended up at the smaller Indiana State in 1976. He quickly became the Sycamores' best player. Bird could score from anywhere on the court. During each of his three seasons at Indiana State, he averaged at least 28 points and 11 rebounds per game. At 6 feet, 9 inches tall, Bird could see over smaller defenders and dish out slick passes.

Basketball fans really took notice of Bird in 1978–79. After an undefeated regular season, the star senior led the Sycamores to their first NCAA Tournament. Once there, Bird sparked a deep run with his dominant scoring and skilled passing. Facing DePaul in the Final Four, Bird recorded 35 points, 16 rebounds, and nine assists. Indiana State won 76–74. In their first-ever NCAA Tournament, the Sycamores were headed to the championship game.

TITANS COLLIDE

Behind legendary coach John Wooden, the University of California, Los Angeles (UCLA), had dominated college basketball in the 1960s and early 1970s. UCLA's star-studded squads drew large audiences. Once Wooden retired in 1975, college basketball needed a new attraction. In 1979, Bird's and Magic's exciting playing styles filled the void.

The 1979 title game took place at Salt Lake City's Special Events Center. More than 35 million people tuned in on television. That made it the most-watched college basketball game ever. Fans were treated to some exciting moments, such as Bird's big steal. But the game turned

Johnson scored 24 points in the 1979 NCAA title game.

into a blowout. Michigan State suffocated Bird and the Sycamores with a well-run zone defense. The national player of the year missed 14 of his 21 shots from the field.

Johnson, meanwhile, showed off his magic skills. In one second-half possession, he cut to the basket just as a pass came his way. He took a dribble then elevated toward the hoop. An Indiana State defender ran into Johnson's path, but it was too late. Johnson threw down a thunderous one-handed dunk through the contact.

With a 75–64 win, Michigan State celebrated its first national title. But the game also marked a victory for the whole of college basketball. Bird and Magic helped draw more fans to the sport, leading to a boom in popularity in the 1980s.

CONTINUED RIVALRY

Bird and Johnson both entered the National Basketball Association (NBA) for the 1979–80 season. The two stars continued to play in big games throughout their pro careers. Johnson's Los Angeles Lakers and Bird's Boston Celtics faced off in the NBA Finals three times during the 1980s. Johnson and the Lakers won two of the three matchups.

CHAPTER TWO

EARLY ICONS

While growing up in Oakland, California, Bill Russell excelled in track and field. He was a dominant sprinter and high jumper. Basketball didn't come quite as naturally. He was cut from his middle school basketball team. His high school coach almost cut him too. Then he had a growth spurt and shot up to 6-foot-5. He also studied other players to improve his own skills.

Russell became an excellent defensive player. Unlike players today, defenders in the 1950s usually didn't jump to contest shots. But Russell wasn't a usual player. Using his high-jumping ability, he soared up for blocks. Even so, nearby University of San Francisco was the only school to offer Russell a basketball scholarship. At the time, freshmen couldn't play on varsity college teams. By his sophomore year, Russell

Bill Russell (6) played on the University of San Francisco's varsity team from 1953–54 to 1955–56.

was 6-foot-10. Once he joined the Dons' varsity squad in 1953–54, Russell transformed the program.

Opposing offenses didn't know how to attack Russell. His quick feet allowed him to guard players on the perimeter. Meanwhile, his height and athleticism allowed him to protect the rim.

As a junior, Russell led San Francisco to the NCAA championship game. The team faced defending champion La Salle and three-time All-America guard Tom Gola. Russell proved to be the best player on the floor. He recorded 23 points and 25 rebounds and lifted the Dons to their first-ever national title.

A year later, San Francisco entered the title game with an undefeated record. Like La Salle, Iowa had no answer for Russell.

Starting in 1959-60, Jerry Lucas (11) averaged 24.3 points per game in three seasons with Ohio State.

He scored 26 points and grabbed 27 rebounds to secure back-to-back championships.

BASKETBALL COMPUTER

Almost every college in the country tried to recruit Jerry Lucas out of high school. The Middleton, Ohio, native had scored the most points in the state's history while leading his team to two state championships. More than 150 colleges offered Lucas a scholarship, but he liked that Ohio State emphasized the importance of academics. So the 6-foot-8 center committed to the Buckeyes.

A straight-A student, Lucas carried his intelligence over to the basketball court. He studied his opponents carefully. Once he learned their strengths and weaknesses, he didn't forget them.

Lucas averaged 26.3 points and 16.4 rebounds per game as a sophomore in 1959–60. No team could slow down the Buckeyes in the NCAA Tournament. Lucas racked up four double-doubles in four games. The Buckeyes won all of their NCAA Tournament games by at least 17 points. They secured the national title with a 75–55 win over California.

Lucas won national player of the year honors as a junior and senior. In those two seasons, the Buckeyes went a combined 53–3. They returned to the national title game in 1961. Lucas put up 27 points and 12 rebounds.

BACK-TO-BACK

In 1946, Oklahoma A&M (now Oklahoma State) senior center Bob Kurland was named the Final Four MOP. That made him the first player to win the award twice. Three years later, Alex Groza of Kentucky matched the feat. The senior center won his second MOP after helping Kentucky defeat Oklahoma A&M in the 1949 title game.

But Ohio State fell to Cincinnati in overtime. Lucas still earned Final Four Most Outstanding Player (MOP) honors. Lucas and the Buckeyes got back to the title game in 1962. However, they once again fell to Cincinnati.

TOWERING UCLA SUPERSTARS

John Wooden coached UCLA to back-to-back national championships in 1964 and 1965. Going into the 1965–66 season, Wooden assembled a star-studded recruiting class headlined by Lew Alcindor. The center started on the freshman team. The first-year players took on the defending national champion varsity team in a scrimmage. Alcindor put up 31 points and 21 rebounds to take down the upperclassmen 75–60.

Alcindor, who later changed his name to Kareem Abdul-Jabbar, joined the varsity team in 1966–67. The 7-foot-2 sophomore scored a school-record 56 points in his first game. Alcindor's towering height and soft touch around the rim made him almost impossible to guard. Using his signature hook shot, "the sky hook," he scored with ease.

UCLA's Lew Alcindor, *left*, grabbed 18 rebounds in the 1967 NCAA title game.

Alcindor led a 26–0 UCLA team into the 1967 NCAA Tournament. Over the next four games, Alcindor averaged 26.5 points and 15.5 rebounds. He scored 20 points in the title game as UCLA beat Dayton 79–64.

The Bruins kept winning in 1967–68. By January 20, 1968, Alcindor was 43–0 with UCLA. Now the team went up against Houston to try for win 44. The meeting between the high-powered teams became known as "The Game of the Century." The Cougars' 71–69 win ended UCLA's streak. But Alcindor got a chance for revenge in the 1968 Final Four. He scored 19 points and grabbed 18 rebounds in the rematch. This time, the Bruins throttled Houston 101–69. The star center went on to score 34 points in a 78–55 championship-game victory over North Carolina.

In 1968–69, UCLA once again rolled to the national championship. Alcindor posted 37 points and 20 rebounds in a 92–72 victory over Purdue. UCLA locked down yet another title. Alcindor left college with more Final Four MOPs (three) than losses (two).

The Bruins won the next two titles after Alcindor graduated. Then, in 1971, another legendary center arrived. The 6-foot-11 Bill Walton regularly scored in the paint. But it was his passing ability that set him apart.

The Bruins went a perfect 60–0 in Walton's first two seasons. He completed the run by going 21 for 22 against

Bill Walton led UCLA to an 87–66 win over Memphis State in the 1973 NCAA title game.

Memphis State in the 1973 title game. Walton finished with 44 points, more than any other player had scored in a national championship game.

Walton's only loss in the NCAA Tournament came in the 1974 Final Four. Walton played all 50 minutes of the game, but his 29 points and 18 rebounds weren't quite enough to snatch a victory. North Carolina State (NC State) ended UCLA's seven-year championship streak in double overtime.

NORTH
23
CAROLINA

CHAPTER THREE

LEGENDS OF MARCH

In 1972, the NCAA began allowing freshmen to play in varsity basketball games. Ten years later, first-year guard Michael Jordan helped North Carolina reach the national championship. Facing Georgetown, the Tar Heels trailed 62–61 with 32 seconds left.

During a timeout, North Carolina coach Dean Smith drew up a play for junior forward James Worthy. However, Smith knew Georgetown would likely double-team Worthy. So the coach told Jordan, "If you get the shot, knock it in."

On the next possession, the Hoyas packed the paint with defenders to deny Worthy. The Tar Heels kicked the ball over to Jordan. The freshman didn't hesitate. He buried a jump shot to give North Carolina

North Carolina's Michael Jordan recorded 16 points and 9 rebounds in the 1982 NCAA championship game.

a one-point lead with 15 seconds left. The Tar Heels held on for the win.

DEFENSIVE FORCE

In 1981, Patrick Ewing was the top recruit in the country. The center's high school coach even compared his elite defensive skills to those of Bill Russell. Ewing arrived at Georgetown for the 1981–82 season. So many people wanted to see the star freshman that the Hoyas started playing in a bigger arena.

Ewing didn't disappoint. The 7-foot, 240-pounder bullied opponents in the paint and anchored a tough defense. He helped the Hoyas reach the 1982 national championship game. Ewing posted 23 points and 11 rebounds. But Georgetown fell to North Carolina 63–62 after Jordan's game-winning shot.

Two years later, Georgetown entered the 1984 NCAA Tournament as one of the favorites. After a first-round bye, the Hoyas got a scare against No. 9 seed Southern Methodist. Late in the game, Ewing tipped in a missed Georgetown free throw to help secure a 37–36 win.

The Hoyas won their next three tournament games by at least 12 points. Facing Houston in the championship game, Ewing blocked four shots. Georgetown won 84–75 to claim its first national title. Ewing's defensive effort earned him a Final Four MOP.

Georgetown's Patrick Ewing (33) recorded 10 points and nine rebounds in the 1984 NCAA title game.

In 1985, Ewing led the No. 1 seed Hoyas back to the championship game. The senior went 7-for-13 from the field. But No. 8 Villanova missed only six shots all game. The Wildcats pulled off the huge upset to deny Ewing another title.

ONE-MAN SHOW

Kansas entered the 1988 NCAA Tournament as a No. 6 seed. No one thought the Jayhawks were the best team before the tournament started. But most fans agreed that the team featured the country's best player. Senior Danny Manning seemed to be everywhere on the court.

The 6-foot, 10-inch forward scored 20 or more points per game in the first four rounds of the tournament. That lifted Kansas to the Final Four. Two years earlier, Duke had beaten Kansas in the national semifinals. The sophomore Manning had scored only four points in that game.

Now the two teams were meeting again in the 1988 Final Four. This time, Manning controlled both ends of the floor. He led all scorers with 25 points. He also added 10 rebounds, six blocks, and four steals. His all-around performance led the Jayhawks to their first title-game appearance in 31 years.

Kansas forward Danny Manning earned national player of the year honors in 1987–88.

Conference rival Oklahoma awaited Kansas in the championship game. The Sooners boasted a fast-paced offense that averaged more than 100 points per game. In the first half, Kansas played at Oklahoma's pace. The Jayhawks regularly turned the ball over but managed to go into halftime tied 50–50.

Kansas coach Larry Brown told his team to play at a much slower pace in the second half. Running a patient offense through Manning, the Jayhawks led 79–77 with 14 seconds left. After one of his teammates missed a free throw, Manning battled for the rebound and got fouled. He made two free throws to extend Kansas's lead. Manning then made two more clutch free throws with five seconds left. The shots secured the championship for Kansas. Manning finished the game with 31 points and a career-high 18 rebounds. Kansas fans remember the unlikely championship team as "Danny and the Miracles."

PERFECT PERFORMANCE

In 1990, Christian Laettner and the Duke Blue Devils lost to the University of Nevada, Las Vegas (UNLV), in the NCAA title game. In the 1991 Final Four, the 6-foot-11 center scored 28 points to get revenge against the Runnin' Rebels. The junior then recorded 18 points and 10 rebounds to lift the Blue Devils to their first national title. Duke beat Kansas 72–65.

Duke's Christian Laettner averaged 19.2 points and 7.8 rebounds per game in the 1992 NCAA Tournament.

Laettner built off that tournament run and won national player of the year honors in 1991–92. He made 58 percent of his field goals, including 56 percent of his three-pointers, both among the nation's best. After helping Duke cruise to the Elite Eight in 1992, Laettner kept showing off his efficient scoring.

Playing against Kentucky, Laettner couldn't miss. The center drilled his first nine shots from the field. And he buried all 10 free throws he took that game. Despite Laettner's perfect shooting, Kentucky took a 103–102 lead with two seconds remaining.

After a timeout, Duke forward Grant Hill inbounded the ball from the Blue Devils' baseline. His pass went 75 feet. Laettner caught the ball at the opposite free-throw line. After taking one dribble, Laettner turned around and released a jump shot. The ball fell through the net as the buzzer sounded. "The Shot" became one of the NCAA Tournament's most iconic plays. Laettner then helped the Blue Devils win their next two games to secure back-to-back championships.

THE FAB FIVE

Juwan Howard, Ray Jackson, Jimmy King, Jalen Rose, and Chris Webber were all top recruits in the 1991 high school class. All five decided to play for Michigan. The "Fab Five" led Michigan to the NCAA title game in 1992 and 1993. The 1992 Wolverines became the first team to start five freshmen in a championship game. However, they fell short that year and again in 1993.

MARQUETTE
3
C-USA
NCAA

2000s STARS

Marquette entered the 2003 NCAA Tournament as a No. 3 seed. It was the school's highest ranking since 1979. In their first game, the Golden Eagles survived an upset attempt from No. 14 seed Holy Cross. After that, Dwyane Wade took over.

The 6-foot, 4-inch guard could drive past defenders with ease. Once he got near the rim, Wade could score through contact. The All-America junior showed off his scoring skills in the next two rounds. He recorded 24 points against Missouri and 22 against Pittsburgh on the way to the Elite Eight.

There, the Golden Eagles faced No. 1 seed Kentucky. Wade did a bit of everything. He regularly set up his teammates to score, racking up 11 assists. He also grabbed 11 rebounds. Late in the second half, Wade got free on a fast break and threw down

Marquette guard Dwyane Wade dribbles past a Missouri defender during the 2003 NCAA Tournament.

a reverse dunk. That slam accounted for two of his 29 points. Wade became one of the few players in NCAA Tournament history to record a triple-double. More importantly, he lifted the Golden Eagles to their first Final Four appearance in 26 years.

FRESHMAN SENSATION

The heroic Wade wasn't even the biggest star of the 2003 NCAA Tournament. Syracuse freshman

Syracuse's Carmelo Anthony averaged 20.2 points and 9.8 rebounds per game in the 2003 NCAA Tournament.

Carmelo Anthony had carried his team all season. The 6-foot-8 forward led the team in scoring and rebounding. Once the tournament started, Anthony didn't shy away from the spotlight.

During Syracuse's first four tournament games, Anthony averaged 17 points and 8.8 rebounds. The star freshman stepped up his game even more in the Final Four. In the semifinals, the forward buried shots from all over the floor. He finished with 33 points, a freshman record in the Final Four. He also added 14 rebounds. Syracuse took down Texas 95–84.

Against Kansas in the championship game, Anthony continued to shine. He recorded team highs with 20 points and 10 rebounds. Meanwhile, his passes got teammates involved. Anthony ended the game with seven assists. Syracuse won 81–78 and secured its first

NEVER NERVOUS

Carmelo Anthony's dominant run as a freshman reminded many college basketball fans of Pervis Ellison. In the 1986 NCAA Tournament, the freshman Ellison helped Louisville make the championship game. "Never Nervous Pervis" made two clutch free throws to give him a game-high 25 points and lift the Cardinals to a national title. Ellison became the first freshman since 1944 to win Final Four MOP.

national title. Anthony became the first freshman since 1986 to win Final Four MOP.

THE OH-FOURS

Al Horford, Joakim Noah, Taurean Green, and Corey Brewer all began playing at Florida in the same year. The talented recruits from the 2004 class called themselves the "Oh-Fours." Off the court, the freshmen quickly grew close with one another. By their sophomore year, their chemistry blossomed on the court.

Coach Billy Donovan wanted his starting five to share the ball and all score the same number of points. The squad's selfless play earned Florida a No. 3 seed in the 2006 NCAA Tournament.

The versatile sophomores shone in the postseason. Horford, a 6-foot-10 forward, grabbed rebounds and scored efficiently. Fellow forward Brewer, who stood 6-foot-9, buried three-pointers. Playing at guard, the 6-foot Green led Florida in assists. And Noah stood out for his overall ability. The 6-foot-11 center led the team in scoring during the tournament with 16.2 points per game. But his intense defense was his biggest strength. Noah blocked 29 shots, the most ever in a single tournament. He also set a title-game record with six blocks. That stifling defense helped the Gators beat UCLA 73–57 to win their first national championship.

Florida's Joakim Noah piled up 21 points, 15 rebounds, and five blocks in the 2006 Elite Eight.

The Oh-Fours could've gone pro on that high note. Instead, they all decided to come back for the 2006–07 season. That was good news for Florida fans. The experienced group made a run back to the 2007 title game. This time, they faced the Ohio State Buckeyes.

Noah was tasked with defending star center Greg Oden. The rest of the Gators looked to shut down the Buckeyes' other scoring threats. When Noah got into foul trouble, Horford and Brewer stepped up on offense. Lifted by six assists from Green, the Gators' forward duo totaled 31 points and 20 rebounds to lead Florida to an 84–75 win. The Gators became the first team in 15 years to repeat as champions.

A STAR IS BORN

Before the 2008 NCAA Tournament, most basketball fans had never heard of Stephen Curry. After all, the sophomore guard played for Davidson. It was a small North Carolina college with fewer than 2,000 students. By the end of the tournament, however, Curry became a household name.

No. 10 seed Davidson faced No. 7 Gonzaga in the first round. Curry started the game hot and never cooled down. With just over a minute to go, the game was tied 74–74. Following a Davidson offensive rebound, Curry buried his eighth three-pointer of the game. The guard finished with 40 points as the Wildcats clinched their first tournament win in 39 years.

No. 2 seed Georgetown presented another tough challenge in the second round. Davidson trailed by 15 early in the second half. Curry then hit a three as a Georgetown player fouled him. That four-point play sparked a comeback for the Wildcats. Curry finished with 30 points as Davidson pulled off the upset.

The Sweet 16 was less dramatic. But Curry still drained deep three-pointers and scored acrobatic layups.

His 33 points helped Davidson take down No. 3 seed Wisconsin 73–56. Facing No. 1 seed Kansas in the Elite Eight, Curry nailed a three to bring the Wildcats within two with under a minute to go. But the Jayhawks held on to win 59–57 and bring an end to Davidson's magical run.

Davidson guard Stephen Curry averaged 5.8 three-pointers per game in the 2008 NCAA Tournament.

UCONN
15

CHAPTER FIVE

MODERN HEROES

Kemba Walker got the mismatch he wanted. A taller, slower defender was guarding the 6-foot-1 guard, and the University of Connecticut (UConn) star quickly went to work. He dribbled hard to his left. Then he leaped back to create space. His defender fell to the floor, leaving Walker open for a jump shot. The ball swished through the net as the buzzer sounded, clinching a UConn victory.

Walker's clutch shot came in the quarterfinals of the 2011 Big East Tournament. March Madness really starts in conference tournaments. They often decide seeding in the NCAA Tournament. Walker led UConn to five wins in five days to clinch the conference title. During that time, he scored a tournament-record 130 points.

UConn guard Kemba Walker (15) averaged 23.5 points per game in 2010–11.

Walker carried the momentum into the NCAA Tournament. In the first round he recorded 18 points, 12 assists, and eight rebounds. Over the next two rounds, Walker added 69 points. He then hit a step-back jumper with just over a minute to go to put the Huskies up five in the Elite Eight. The clutch shot from "Cardiac Kemba" helped UConn advance to the Final Four. There, Walker averaged 17 points and 7.5 rebounds per game to lead the Huskies to the national title.

FROM KEMBA TO SHABAZZ

Walker stole all of the headlines during the 2011 NCAA Tournament. But freshman Shabazz Napier also played a key role in getting the Huskies to the championship game. During the semifinal against Kentucky, Napier secured a rebound with three seconds to go. The 6-foot-1 guard then buried two free throws to ice the game.

Three years later, Napier led the team in scoring as a senior. Entering the 2014 NCAA Tournament as a No. 7 seed, UConn wasn't expected to make a deep run. The Huskies almost lost in the first round. They needed every one of Napier's 24 points, eight rebounds, and six assists to take down Saint Joseph's in overtime.

In six tournament games, the crafty Napier averaged 21.2 points, 5.5 rebounds, and 4.5 assists. That included a game-high 22 points in the championship game

Shabazz Napier (13) scored 25 points in UConn's 60–54 victory over Michigan State in the 2014 Elite Eight.

against Kentucky. For the second time in four years, a high-scoring point guard led UConn to a championship.

BLOCK PARTY

In the early 2010s, Kentucky was also making deep runs in the NCAA Tournament. Each year, Kentucky coach John Calipari built his teams around top high school recruits. Those star freshmen typically turned into high NBA Draft picks the following year. But the Wildcats hadn't won a championship in years.

Anthony Davis wanted to change that. The top recruit in the country in 2011, Davis stood 6 feet, 10 inches tall. He used his height and lengthy wingspan to swat

Kentucky's Anthony Davis averaged 13.7 points, 12.3 rebounds, and 4.8 blocks per game during the 2012 NCAA Tournament.

away shots. After leading the country in blocks during the regular season in 2011–12, the forward took his defensive game to a new level in the NCAA Tournament. In the first round, Davis blocked seven shots. Behind their defensive anchor, the Wildcats made a run to the Final Four.

Facing in-state rival Louisville in the semifinals, Davis showcased his all-around game. He was dominant on defense as usual, blocking five shots. Meanwhile, on offense, he went 7-for-8 from the field and scored a game-high 18 points. He also added 14 rebounds as Kentucky moved on to the championship game. Davis missed nine of his 10 shots in the title game. However, his defensive impact made up for the poor shooting. He matched Joakim Noah's championship-game record of six blocks. The star freshman helped Kentucky take down Kansas 67–59 to win the national title.

SCORING MACHINE

Entering the 2023 NCAA Tournament, Purdue earned a No. 1 seed for the first time since 1996. Junior Zach Edey was the main reason why. Opponents struggled to handle the 7-foot-4 center. However, No. 16 seed Fairleigh Dickinson shocked Purdue in the first round of the tournament, beating the Boilermakers 63–58. The Knights became just the second No. 16 seed in men's tournament history to beat a No. 1 seed.

Purdue center Zach Edey recorded 40 points and 16 rebounds in the 2024 Elite Eight.

Edey bounced back in 2023–24. The senior led the country in scoring that season. Purdue once again entered the NCAA Tournament as a No. 1 seed. And Edey wasn't about to let another upset happen. He racked up 30 points and 21 rebounds to lead Purdue to a 78–50 blowout win over Grambling State.

Edey continued to punish opponents in the paint throughout the tournament. He recorded at least 20 points and 10 rebounds in the first five games. Edey's dominance lifted the Boilermakers to their first championship appearance since 1969. There, UConn didn't have many answers for the star center. Edey made 60 percent of his shots and finished with 37 points. However, Edey's teammates struggled to score. UConn came away with a 75–60 win. Even so, Edey became the first person since 1983 to earn national player of the year honors two years in a row.

COMEBACK KID

With under three minutes left in the 2025 Elite Eight, Florida trailed Texas Tech 75–66. Walter Clayton Jr. then hit a pair of three-pointers to spark a comeback win. The senior guard finished the game with 30 points. In the Final Four, Clayton Jr. scored a season-high 34 points against Auburn. No player had recorded back-to-back 30-point games that late in the tournament since Indiana State's Larry Bird in 1979. In the championship game, Houston slowed down Clayton Jr. in the first half. The guard scored all 11 of his points in the second half. He helped the Gators overcome a 12-point deficit to win the national title.

HONORABLE MENTIONS

GAIL GOODRICH

UCLA guard Goodrich averaged 35 points per game in the 1965 NCAA Tournament, finishing the run with a then-record 42 points in the championship game against Michigan.

DAVID THOMPSON

In 1974, NC State junior forward Thompson scored 28 points in the Final Four to end UCLA's 38-game NCAA Tournament winning streak. The Wolfpack finished the job in the championship game, beating Marquette to win the title.

Kris Jenkins

ISIAH THOMAS

In the 1981 NCAA Tournament, Thomas racked up a then-record 43 assists for Indiana. The sophomore guard scored a game-high 23 points in the title game to lift the Hoosiers over North Carolina 63–50.

Hakeem Olajuwon

HAKEEM OLAJUWON

Olajuwon, a 7-foot center, led Houston to the NCAA championship game in 1983 and 1984. In those two tournaments, Olajuwon averaged 19.1 points, 12.2 rebounds, and 4.6 blocks per game.

KRIS JENKINS

Villanova and North Carolina were tied 74–74 with 4.7 seconds left in the 2016 national-title game. Just before the final buzzer sounded, Villanova forward Jenkins released a three-pointer. He buried the shot to win the championship for the Wildcats.

TRISTEN NEWTON

Newton transferred to UConn before the 2022–23 season. In his two years with the Huskies, the guard won two national championships. Newton led the Huskies in scoring in both title games and earned Final Four Most Outstanding Player honors in 2024.

GLOSSARY

alley-oop
When a player catches a pass in the air and scores before coming down to the floor.

clutch
Performing well in an important situation that often decides a competition or game.

conference
A group of schools that join together to create a league for their sports teams.

draft
A system that allows teams to acquire new players coming into a league.

fast break
A time when players move the ball up the floor quickly.

hook shot
A shot taken above a player's head when they are positioned sideways to the basket.

paint
The area in the middle of the court between the baseline and the free-throw line.

rival
An opponent with whom a player or team has a fierce and ongoing competition.

scholarship
Money awarded to a student to pay for education expenses.

triple-double
Accumulating 10 or more of three certain statistics in a game.

upset
An unexpected victory by a supposedly weaker team or player.

varsity
A school's top team.

versatile
Able to perform many different roles or functions.

MORE INFORMATION

BOOKS

Giedd, Steph. *Basketball Strategies.* Abdo, 2024.

Mahoney, Brian. *GOATs of Basketball.* Abdo, 2022.

Monnig, Alex. *Basketball.* Abdo, 2023.

ONLINE RESOURCES

To learn more about March Madness men's superstars, please visit **abdobooklinks.com** or scan this QR code. These links are routinely monitored and updated to provide the most current information available.

INDEX

ABOUT THE AUTHOR

Luke Hanlon is a sportswriter and editor who lives in Minneapolis, Minnesota. He's written dozens of nonfiction books for kids and spends a lot of his free time watching his favorite Minnesota sports teams.